Baritone/Bass Volume 4
Book/Accompaniment

THE SINGERS MUSICAL THEATRE ANTHOLOGY

A collection of songs from the musical stage, categorized by voice type. The selections are presented in their authentic settings, excerpted from the original vocal scores.

Compiled and Edited by Richard Walters

ISBN-13: 978-1-4234-2382-9
ISBN-10: 1-4234-2382-8

7777 W. BLUEMOUND RD. P.O. BOX 13819 MILWAUKEE, WI 53213

For all works contained herein:
Unauthorized copying, arranging, adapting, recording or public performance is an infringement of copyright.
Infringers are liable under the law.

Visit Hal Leonard Online at
www.halleonard.com

Foreword
to the original edition

When I conceived and compiled the first volumes of *The Singer's Musical Theatre Anthology*, released in 1987, I couldn't have possibly imagined the day when I would be writing the foreword for Volume 4. Such a venture is made possible only by the lively and sustained interest of singing actors of all descriptions, be they students or professionals. As a researcher I can only present you with practical choices from existing theatre literature. Without the dedicated pursuit of that music by people such as you, dear reader, these collections would remain on a shelf, unopened.

Volume 4 allows inclusion of songs from shows opened since Volume 3 (released in 2000), as well as a continuing, deeper look into both classic and contemporary musical theatre repertory. As has been the case with each of the solo voice volumes in this series, songs are chosen with many types of talent in mind. All songs do not suit all singers. It is good and natural for any performer to stretch as far as possible, attempting diverse material. But it is also very important ultimately to know what you do well. That is an individual answer, based on your voice, your temperament and your look. This collection has enough variety of songs that any interested performer should be able to find several viable choices.

You will come up with a more individual interpretation, conjured from the ground up in the manner that all the best actors work, if you learn a song on your own, building it into your unique singing voice, *without* imitating a recorded performance. Particularly try to avoid copying especially famous renditions of a song, because you can probably only suffer in the comparison. Would you learn a role from Shakespeare, Shaw or Edward Albee solely by mimicking a recording, film or video/DVD of it? Your answer had better be *of course not!* The same needs to be true of theatre music. After you know the notes and lyrics very well, study the character's stated and unstated motivations and thoughts to come up with your own performance. Explore your own ideas about musical and vocal phrasing to express the character's emotions. In other words, make a song your own, and no one can take it away from you. It's yours for life.

Original keys are used exclusively in this edition. Sometimes these reflect the composer's musical/vocal concept, and sometimes they are merely the keys best suited to the original performers. Still, they give a singer a very good idea of the desired vocal timbre for a song as presented in its authentic theatre context. There are general vocal guidelines for voice types in theatre music, but these are not in stone. A soprano with a good belt will be able to sing songs from the soprano volumes as well as the mezzo-soprano/belter volumes. Belters may decide to work on their "head voice" in soprano songs. Men who have voices that lie between tenor and baritone, commonly called "baritenors" (a common range in contemporary musical theatre), may find songs in both the tenor and baritone/bass volumes.

In my foreword for Volume 3 of *The Singer's Musical Theatre Anthology*, written in 2000, I stated that the movie musical was dead. What a difference five years makes! The genre appears to be gaining a little steam at this writing, evidence of the continued relevance of musical theatre to a wider audience.

The books comprising Volume 4 of this series would not have been possible without the enthusiastic help of Brian Dean as assistant editor, and I thank him heartily.

All the selections from all volumes of this series, including duets, total nearly 700 songs. A marathon performance of all the songs in all volumes of *The Singer's Musical Theatre Anthology* would take more than 40 hours. What fun that would be!

Richard Walters,
December, 2005

THE SINGER'S MUSICAL THEATRE ANTHOLOGY
Baritone/Bass Volume 4

Contents

Disc One

Track	Page	
		ALLEGRO
1	14	A Fellow Needs a Girl [3]
		ANNIE GET YOUR GUN
2	17	I'm a Bad, Bad Man [3]
		ASPECTS OF LOVE
3	22	Other Pleasures [3]
		AVENUE Q
4	34	What Do You Do with a B.A. in English? [1]
5	26	I'm Not Wearing Underwear Today [1]
6	28	Fantasies Come True [1]
		BIG RIVER
7	46	Waitin' for the Light to Shine [3]
		BYE BYE BIRDIE
8	37	Put on a Happy Face [2]
9	42	A Lot of Livin' to Do [2]
		LA CAGE AUX FOLLES
10	48	Masculinity [2]
		CAMELOT
11	54	I Wonder What the King Is Doing Tonight [2]
		ELEGIES FOR ANGELS, PUNKS, AND RAGING QUEENS
12	68	Heroes All Around [1]
		FOLLIES
13	72	The Right Girl [2]
		A FUNNY THING HAPPENED ON THE WAY TO THE FORUM
14	61	Bring Me My Bride [2]
		GREASE
15	84	Greased Lightnin' [1]
		I LOVE YOU, YOU'RE PERFECT, NOW CHANGE
16	94	Shouldn't I Be Less in Love with You? [3]
		JOSEPH AND THE AMAZING TECHNICOLOR® DREAMCOAT
17	89	Those Canaan Days [3]
		LOUISIANA PURCHASE
18	100	What Chance Have I with Love? [3]
		MILK AND HONEY
19	104	There's No Reason in the World [3]
		MONTY PYTHON'S SPAMALOT
20	122	Always Look on the Bright Side of Life [1]

Disc Two

Track	Page	
		THE MUSIC MAN
1	109	Ya Got Trouble [2]
		MY FAIR LADY
2	136	With a Little Bit of Luck [2]
3	128	Get Me to the Church on Time [3]
		PAINT YOUR WAGON
4	156	Wand'rin' Star [3]
		THE PRODUCERS
5	150	In Old Bavaria [3]
6	145	Along Came Bialy [3]
7	152	Haben Sie Gehört Das Deutsche Band? (Have You Ever Heard the German Band?) [4]
		RAGTIME
8	162	Make Them Hear You [2]
		THE RINK
9	166	Marry Me [3]
		THE ROAR OF THE GREASEPAINT—THE SMELL OF THE CROWD
10	169	A Wonderful Day Like Today [3]
11	176	Who Can I Turn To? (When Nobody Needs Me) [4]
		1776
12	180	Molasses to Rum [2]
		THE SOUND OF MUSIC
13	192	Edelweiss [3]
		WICKED
14	195	Wonderful [3]
		THE WILD PARTY
15	204	I'll Be Here [2]
		WISH YOU WERE HERE
16	208	Relax [3]
		WOMAN OF THE YEAR
17	212	Sometimes a Day Goes By [3]
		WONDERFUL TOWN
18	220	A Quiet Girl [4]
19	215	It's Love [3]
		YOU'RE A GOOD MAN, CHARLIE BROWN
20	226	The Kite (Charlie Brown's Kite) [2]

Pianists on the CDs:

[1] Brian Dean
[2] Ruben Piirainen
[3] Christopher Ruck
[4] Richard Walters

ABOUT THE SHOWS

The material in this section is by Stanley Green, Richard Walters, Brian Dean, and Robert Viagas, some of which was previously published elsewhere.

ALLEGRO

MUSIC: Richard Rogers
LYRICS AND BOOK: Oscar Hammerstein II
DIRECTOR AND CHOREOGRAPHER: Agnes de Mille
OPENED: 10/10/47, New York; a run of 315 performances

Allegro was the third Rogers and Hammerstein musical on Broadway and the first with a story that had not been based on a previous source. It was a an ambitious undertaking, with its theme of the corrupting effect of big institutions told through the life of a doctor, Joseph Taylor, Jr., from his birth in a small American town to his thirty-fifth year. Joe grows up, goes to school, marries a local belle, joins the staff of a large Chicago hospital that panders to wealthy patients, discovers that his wife is unfaithful and, in the end, returns to his midwestern home town with his adoring nurse to dedicate himself to healing the sick and helping the needy. One innovation in the musical was the use of a Greek chorus to comment on the action and sing directly to the actors and the audience. Joseph's father and mother sit on the porch, dreaming of their son's future loves, and remembering their own in "A Fellow Needs a Girl."

ANNIE GET YOUR GUN

MUSIC AND LYRICS: Irving Berlin
BOOK: Herbert Fields and Dorothy Fields
DIRECTOR: Joshua Logan
CHOREOGRAPHER: Helen Tamiris
OPENED: 5/16/46, New York; a run of 1,147 performances

Irving Berlin's musical biography of scrappy gal sharpshooter Annie Oakley earned standing ovations for Broadway stars of two generations: the original, Ethel Merman, in the 1940s; and Bernadette Peters in the 1990s. The tune-packed musical traces Annie's rise from illiterate hillbilly to international marksmanship star as she's discovered and developed in the traveling "Buffalo Bill's Wild West Show." She falls hard for the show's chauvinistic male star, Frank Butler, whose wily ways are introduced in "I'm a Bad, Bad Man." And romance blossoms—right up until Annie begins to outshine Frank. In the end, after quarrelling, the two get married. The movie version was originally to have starred Judy Garland, but after she was fired from the set, Betty Hutton played the role opposite Howard Keel in the 1950 release. The major Broadway revival starring Peters opened in 1999; Reba McEntire also enjoyed special acclaim as Annie in that production.

ASPECTS OF LOVE

MUSIC: Andrew Lloyd Webber
LYRICS: Don Black and Charles Hart
BOOK: Andrew Lloyd Webber
DIRECTOR: Trevor Nunn
CHOREOGRAPHER: Gillian Lynne
OPENED: 4/8/90, New York; a run of 377 performances

Aspects of Love is based on an autobiographical novel by David Garnett, a nephew of Virginia Woolf. The show had an intimate production style, with orchestrations that threw out the brass in favor of a chamber music sound. It follows a group of characters over nearly two decades of interweaving relationships. The story begins with a 17-year-old boy, Alex, who is infatuated with an actress, Rose, in her mid-20s. The actress eventually has a love affair with Alex's uncle George, and they marry. Along the way almost everyone winds up in love with, or broken-hearted by, all the others. The plot is emotionally complex, as are the characters and their relationships. Rose and George have a beautiful daughter, Jenny. George is an older and worldly man, but he would trade all the "Other Pleasures" in his life for his young daughter.

AVENUE Q

MUSIC AND LYRICS: Robert Lopez and Jeff Marx
BOOK: Jeff Whitty
DIRECTOR: Jason Moore
CHOREOGRAPHER: Ken Roberson
OPENED: 7/31/03, New York; still running as of December 2005

Avenue Q is an ironic homage to *Sesame Street*, though the puppet characters are much more adult, dealing with topics such as loud lovemaking, closeted homosexuality, and internet porn addiction. The puppeteers are onstage, acting and singing for their characters, but there are also humans in the production. The story deals with a young college graduate, Princeton, who learns how to live life and find love in New York. Along the way we meet the many tenants in his in his apartment building on Avenue Q. At the outset, Princeton, like many liberal arts majors, wonders "What Do You Do with a B.A. in English?" On a date at a club, Princeton and Kate Monster are awed by Brian's opening standup number "I'm Not Wearing Underwear Today." Rod and Nicky are Ernie and Bert spoofs. The closeted Bert character Rod dreams of a day when he can have Nicky for himself in "Fantasies Come True."

BIG RIVER

MUSIC AND LYRICS: Roger Miller
BOOK: William Hauptman
DIRECTOR: Des McAnuff
CHOREOGRAPHER: Janet Watson
OPENED: 4/25/85, New York; a run of 1,005 performances

The show is based on Mark Twain's classic novel, *The Adventures of Huckleberry Finn*, about an early 19th-century Missouri boy who tries to help a runaway slave escape to the North, but accidentally winds up riding with him on a raft down the Mississippi into the deep South. Along the way they explore a country full of fraud and hate, but also full of innocence and even beauty. The show featured a score from country songwriter Roger Miller ("King of the Road"). As the title suggests, *Big River* evokes the Mississippi as constantly present, almost as a character in the play. Practically an orphan already due to his no good father, Huck longs for something better in his young life, having spent too much time already "Waitin' for the Light to Shine."

BYE BYE BIRDIE

MUSIC: Charles Strouse
LYRICS: Lee Adams
BOOK: Michael Stewart
DIRECTOR AND CHOREOGRAPHER: Gower Champion
OPENED: 4/14/60, New York; a run of 607 performances

The first musical to deal with rock and roll and its effect on the youth, *Bye Bye Birdie* was also the first musical by writers Charles Strouse and Lee Adams. Conrad Birdie is the Elvis-inspired pop star who is being drafted. As a publicity stunt before he leaves for the army, his agent Albert decides that he will kiss a young lady live on the Ed Sullivan television show while performing his new song "One Last Kiss." The ingenue of his affection is teenager Kim McAffee. Birdie and Albert are boarding a train to go to Ohio and meet Kim; Albert has to sing "Put On a Happy Face" to the lovelorn girls who have flocked to the depot to see their idol leave town. Tempers flare when Kim's current romance is tread upon, and Birdie is punched out while on the air by her jealous boyfriend before the singer can plant the kiss on Kim. After that fiasco, Birdie wants to let loose at a local night spot, insisting that before he goes off to the army he has "A Lot of Livin' to Do." Later on, a chase ensues as Birdie tries to get out of town. The original production starred Dick Van Dyke, Chita Rivera, Kay Medford and Charles Nelson Reilly. The 1963 movie starred Van Dyke, Janet Leigh, Maureen Stapleton, Paul Lynde, and Ann-Margret. A TV version was made in 1995 with Jason Alexander, Vanessa Williams, and Chynna Phillips. A sequel, *Bring Back Birdie*, by the same authors, had a short run in 1981.

LA CAGE AUX FOLLES

MUSIC AND LYRICS: Jerry Herman
BOOK: Harvey Fierstein, based on the play by Jean Poiret
DIRECTOR: Arthur Laurents
CHOREOGRAPHER: Scott Salmon
OPENED: 8/21/83, New York; a run of 1,761 performances

French author Jean Poiret's successful play and film about the relationship between the owner of a St. Tropez drag-queen nightclub and his star attraction provided Harvey Fierstein and Jerry Herman material for a Broadway musical. In the story, the flamboyant Albin (George Hearn)—known on the stage as Zaza—and the more conservative Georges (Gene Barry) are middle-aged lovers who have been together for over 20 years. Their domestic peace is shattered, however, when Jean-Michel, Georges' son as a result of a youthful indiscretion, tells his father that he plans to wed the daughter of Edouard Dindon, a local morals crusader. In order for Georges to appear to his future in-laws as an upstanding citizen, he agrees that Albin must somehow be put back into the closet, a task he undertakes in "Masculinity." Though hurt and defiant, Albin swallows his pride and aids the deception by dressing up as Georges' wife. After inadvertently revealing who he really is, Albin is not above a little blackmail to force Dindon to permit the marriage to take place. A revival was staged in 2004. The film *The Birdcage* is an adaptation of the same story.

CAMELOT

MUSIC: Frederick Loewe
LYRICS AND BOOK: Alan Jay Lerner
DIRECTOR: Moss Hart
CHOREOGRAPHER: Hanya Holm
OPENED: 12/3/60, New York; for a run of 873 performances

Lerner and Loewe's Broadway production following their spectacular hit, *My Fair Lady*, was another musical based on a highly esteemed work of British fiction, T.H. White's novel, *The Once and Future King*. Again, too, they were joined by fair lady Julie Andrews and director Moss Hart for an opulently mounted retelling of the Arthurian legend, with its high-minded knights of the round table and its tragic romantic triangle involving King Arthur, his queen Guenevere, and his trusted knight, Sir Lancelot. Surprisingly enough, Arthur is a mess the night before his marriage to Guenevere, who he has just met incognito. He playfully muses about what the commoners must be thinking about him in "I Wonder What the King is Doing Tonight."

ELEGIES FOR ANGELS, PUNKS, AND RAGING QUEENS

MUSIC: Janet Hood
LYRICS AND BOOK: Bill Russell
DIRECTION AND STAGING: Bill Russell
OPENED: first performance 5/89, New York

Composer/lyricist Bill Russell was extremely moved when the Names Project Quilt was unveiled in Washington, DC in 1987, memorializing those dead from AIDS. A fan of the Edgar Lee Masters collection of poetry the *Spoon River Anthology*, where members in a cemetery recite their own epitaphs, Russell set out to create his own show, told in the words and stories of AIDS patients, which celebrates life and love, struggle and hope. The show, often given in conjunction with AIDS awareness and fundraising, has been performed in several countries, including the U.K., Germany, Sweden, Israel and Australia. A recording was made of the all-star performance given in New York in April, 2001, to benefit the Momentum AIDS Project. Some of the songs have a gospel feel to them. The altruistic actions of many unnamed good souls is celebrated in "Heroes All Around."

FOLLIES

MUSIC AND LYRICS: Stephen Sondheim
BOOK: James Goldman
DIRECTION: Harold Prince and Michael Bennett
CHOREOGRAPHER: Michael Bennett
OPENED: 4/4/71, New York; a run of 522 performances

Follies takes place at a reunion of former Ziegfeld Follies-type showgirls on the night before the destruction of the theatre where they all once played. The musical deals with the reality of life as contrasted with the unreality of the theatre and the past. *Follies* explores this theme through the lives of two couples, the upper-class, unhappy, Phyllis and Benjamin Stone, and the middle-class, also unhappy, Sally and Buddy Plummer. *Follies* also shows us these four as they were in their pre-marital youth. The young actors appear as ghosts to haunt their elder selves. Because the show is about the past, and often in cinematically inspired flashback, Sondheim styled his songs to evoke some of the theatre's great composers and lyricists of the past. Buddy's quest in life is to find "The Right Girl." He realizes in the frenetic song that perhaps he has made the wrong choice.

A FUNNY THING HAPPENED ON THE WAY TO THE FORUM

MUSIC AND LYRICS: Stephen Sondheim
BOOK: Burt Shevelove and Larry Gelbart
DIRECTOR: George Abbott
CHOREOGRAPHER: Jack Cole
OPENED: 5/8/62, New York; a run of 964 performances

Full of sight gags, pratfalls, mistaken identity, leggy girls, and other familiar vaudeville ingredients, *Forum* is a bawdy, farcical, pell-mell musical whose likes have seldom been seen on Broadway. Originally intended as a vehicle first for Phil Silvers and then for Milton Berle, *A Funny Thing Happened on the Way to the Forum* opened on Broadway with Zero Mostel as Pseudolus the slave, who is forced to go through a series of mad-cap adventures before being allowed his freedom. Though the show was a hit, things had not looked very promising during the pre-Broadway tryout, and director Jerome Robbins was called in. The most important change: beginning the musical with the song "Comedy Tonight," which set the right mood for the wacky doings that followed. To come up with a script, the librettists researched all twenty-one surviving comedies by the Roman playwright Plautus (254-184 BC), then wrote an original book incorporating such typical characters as the conniving servants, the lascivious master, the domineering mistress, the officious warrior, the simple-minded hero (called Hero), and the senile old man. Vain warrior Miles Gloriosus, back from the spoils of war, wants another as well—he calls to his soldiers, "Bring Me My Bride." Both Mostel (as Pseudolus) and Silvers (as Marcus Lycus) were in the 1966 United Artists screen version, along with Jack Gilford and Buster Keaton. The 1997 Broadway revival starred Nathan Lane as Pseudolus; the role was later played by Whoopi Goldberg.

GREASE

MUSIC, LYRICS AND BOOK: Jim Jacobs and Warren Casey
DIRECTOR: Tom Moore
CHOREOGRAPHER: Patricia Birch
OPENED: 2/14/72, New York; a run of 3,388 performances

A surprise runaway hit reflecting the nostalgia fashion of the 1970s, *Grease* is the story of hip greaser Danny Zuko and his wholesome girl Sandy Dumbrowski, a loose plot that serves as an excuse for a light-hearted ride through the early rock and roll of the 1950s. The 1978 movie version, starring John Travolta and Olivia Newton-John, is one of the top grossing movie musicals of all time. A hit revival opened in 1994, with a revolving Rizzo, played by Rosie O'Donnell, Brook Shields, Lucy Lawless and Debbie Gibson, among others. Motorhead Kinickie supes up his car "Greased Lightnin'" to impress his boys and attract the girls.

I LOVE YOU, YOU'RE PERFECT, NOW CHANGE

MUSIC: Jimmy Roberts
LYRICS AND BOOK: Joe DiPietro
DIRECTOR: Joel Bishoff
OPENED: 8/1/95, New York; still running as of December 2005

This sleeper hit Off-Broadway revue addresses the whole messy process of being single, dating, finding romance, picking a mate, marrying, having children, having affairs, trying to rekindle the spark in marriage, etc. Though simple in its conception, the show found its niche as a good "date" musical, sailing past 3,000 performances in 2005, and seeing productions in cities around the world. After thirty years of sometimes rocky marriage, a man looks back, and asks of his wife, "Shouldn't I Be Less in Love with You?" His answer, despite all their trials, is a resounding no.

JOSEPH AND THE AMAZING TECHNICOLOR® DREAMCOAT

MUSIC: Andrew Lloyd Webber
LYRICS AND BOOK: Tim Rice
OPENED: 5/12/68, London
　　　　　　1/27/82, New York; a run of 747 performances

The musical lasted all of 15 minutes in its first form, written for a school production in 1968, the first produced collaboration by the young Andrew Lloyd Webber and Tim Rice. By 1973 the piece had been expanded to about 90 minutes, and was staged in the West End. The first New York performance took place at the Brooklyn Academy of Music in 1976, and a Broadway run finally commenced in 1981. Somewhat of a forerunner to the biblically based *Jesus Christ Superstar*, Joseph is told entirely in an eclectic mix of rock, country, vaudeville and calypso song styles. Drawn from the Old Testament, the musical tells the story of Joseph, Jacob's favorite of 12 sons, who is given a remarkable coat of many colors. His jealous brothers sell him into slavery, and he is taken to Egypt, where he interprets the dream of Pharaoh. His wise prophecy so impresses Pharaoh that Joseph is elevated in honor and position, and put in charge of saving the country from famine. His brothers, meanwhile, have fallen onto hard times; Reuben reminisces about "Those Canaan Days" when life was good. The show has a joyous climax, with the reunion of Joseph and his family.

LOUISIANA PURCHASE

MUSIC AND LYRICS: Irving Berlin
BOOK: Morrie Ryskind, based on a story by B.G. DeSylva
DIRECTOR: Edgar MacGregor
CHOREOGRAPHY: George Balanchine, Carl Randall
OPENED: 5/28/40, New York; a run of 444 performances

Inspired by the corruption in Huey Long's governorship of Louisiana, Berlin's first musical since 1933's *As Thousands Cheer* dealt with the fictional investigation squeaky-clean Senator Oliver P. Loganberry makes of the Louisiana Purchasing Company. Jim Taylor, the company's president, tries to block the probe by involving the incorruptible Senator first with Marina Van Linden, a Viennese refugee, then with Mme. Yvonne Bordelaise, a local restaurateuse. Longanberry manages to get out of the trap by marrying Yvonne, but he is ultimately defeated when, being a politician, he is unwilling to cross the picket line in front of the building in which his hearing is to take place. "What Chance Have I with Love?" is a comic lament of an insecure man; if love could bring down mighty Anthony, his own chances are slim. The first recording of this show was made in 1996 with the cast of a New York performance, featuring the original Rodney Russell Bennett orchestrations.

MILK AND HONEY

MUSIC AND LYRICS: Jerry Herman
BOOK: Don Appell
DIRECTOR: Albert Marre
CHOREOGRAPHER: Donald Saddler
OPENED: 10/10/61, New York; a run of 543 performances

Milk and Honey was Jerry Herman's first Broadway show. Generally about American tourists in Israel, the show relates the ill-fated romance of a middle-aged businessman, Phil, and a younger woman, Ruth, who cannot overcome her qualms about a liaison with a married man. Phil tries to assuage her fears by letting her know "There's No Reason in the World" that the two of them can't be together.

MONTY PYTHON'S SPAMALOT

MUSIC: John Du Prez and Eric Idle
LYRICS: Eric Idle
BOOK: Eric Idle, "lovingly ripped off from the motion picture *Monty Python and the Holy Grail*"
DIRECTOR: Mike Nichols
CHOREOGRAPHER: Casey Nicholaw
OPENED: 3/17/05, New York, still running as of

Eric Idle, one of the founding members of the British television comedy troupe "Monty Python's Flying Circus," made his Broadway writing debut with *Monty Python's Spamalot*, billed as "a new musical lovingly ripped off from the motion picture *Monty Python and the Holy Grail*." As in the movie, the show involves the wacky adventures of King Arthur and his band of knights in their search for the Holy Grail, shrubbery, and in the musical, success on the Great White Way. *Spamalot* is a lavish production, featuring a large cast and sets, and directed by luminary Broadway and movie director Mike Nichols. The original cast starred Tim Curry, Hank Azaria, and David Hyde Pierce. True to characteristic Python irreverence and silliness, *Spamalot* lambasts the musical genre at every step. Originally written as a song for the Jesus-like character to sing *on* the cross in the movie *The Life of Brian*, "Always Look on the Bright Side of Life" works in the stage show as a picker-upper, sung by Patsy, for Arthur and the Knights.

THE MUSIC MAN

MUSIC, LYRICS AND BOOK: Meredith Willson
DIRECTOR: Morton Da Costa
CHOREOGRAPHER: Onna White
OPENED: 12/19/57, New York; a run of 1,375 performances

With *The Music Man*, composer-lyricist-librettist Meredith Willson recaptured the innocent charm of the middle American town where he grew up (Mason City, Iowa). It is the Fourth of July, 1912, and the abundantly charming "Professor" Harold Hill, actually a traveling con man, arrives in River City, Iowa, ready to work his scam. First, he whips the town into a fury, playing them into his hands, when he discusses the disaster indicated by the presence of a pool table in their community in "Ya Got Trouble." He then poses as a professor of music, collecting money for lessons and instruments on the promise that he can keep the town's children on the straight and narrow while teaching them how to play in a band through his fraudulent "Think System." But his plans to pocket the cash and skip town are complicated by the presence of the temptingly pretty Marian Paroo, the librarian and music teacher. She sees through him immediately, but is soon won over by the palpable excitement he's able to generate among the stuffy townspeople, and in her formerly withdrawn younger brother. The story ends with a touch of theatre magic. Just as the townspeople are about to tar and feather Hill, lo and behold, the "Think System" works, and the kids are able to play…sort of. The show, which took eight years and more than thirty rewrites before it was produced on Broadway, marked Willson's auspicious debut in the theatre. It was also the first musical-stage appearance by Robert Preston, playing the role of Harold Hill, who went on to repeat his dynamic performance in the 1962 Warner Bros. screen version. A 1980 Broadway revival starred Dick Van Dyke. Another Broadway revival opened in 2001. Matthew Broderick and Kristin Chenoweth starred in the 2003 television production.

MY FAIR LADY

MUSIC: Frederick Loewe
LYRICS AND BOOK: Alan Jay Lerner
DIRECTOR: Moss Hart
CHOREOGRAPHER: Hanya Holm
OPENED: 3/15/56, New York, a run of 2,717 performances

The most celebrated musical of the 1950s began as an idea of Hungarian film producer Gabriel Pascal, who devoted the last two years of his life trying to find writers to adapt George Bernard Shaw's play, *Pygmalion*, into a stage musical. The team of Lerner and Loewe also saw the possibilities, particularly when they realized that they could use most of the original dialogue and simply expand the action to include scenes at the Ascot Races and Embassy Ball. They were also scrupulous in maintaining the Shavian flavor in their songs, most apparent in such pieces as "Get Me to the Church on Time," "Why Can't the English?," "Show Me" and "Without You." Shaw was concerned that British society had become so stratified and segregated that different classes had developed their own separate accents. His social observation was dramatized in the story of Eliza Doolittle (originated in the musical by Julie Andrews), a scruffy flower seller in London's Covent Garden, who takes speech lessons from Prof. Henry Higgins (Rex Harrison) so that she might qualify for the position of a florist in a shop. Eliza succeeds so well that she outgrows her social station and—in a development added by librettist Lerner—even makes Higgins fall in love with her. Three revivals have been mounted in New York, including Harrison's return in 1981. Harrison and Audrey Hepburn (whose singing was dubbed by Marni Nixon) were seen in the 1964 Warner Bros. movie version, directed by George Cukor. Eliza's rough, convivial father Albert has a couple of showstoppers. Early on, he celebrates his carefree life, skimmed through "With a Little Bit of Luck." Later on, Higgins influences a philanthropist to will money to Doolittle; yanked into middle class respectability with his wealth, he must marry his longtime female chum to keep up appearances ("Get Me to the Church on Time").

PAINT YOUR WAGON

MUSIC: Fredrick Loewe
LYRICS AND BOOK: Alan Jay Lerner
CHOREOGRAPHER: Agnes De Mille
DIRECTOR: Daniel Mann
OPENED: 11/21/51, New York; a run of 289 performances

Filling their musical with historical incidents and backgrounds, Lerner and Loewe created a work that captured the flavor of roistering, robust California gold prospectors of 1853. Ben Rumson is a grizzled prospector whose daughter Jennifer discovers gold near their camp. Word of the strike quickly spreads and before long there are over 40,000 inhabitants in the new town of Rumson. Jennifer, who has fallen in love with Julio, a Mexican, goes East to school but returns to Julio when the gold peters out. Ben contemplates leaving Rumson, pointing out he was born under a "Wan'drin' Star," but will eventually stay in what becomes a ghost town, left with nothing but his hopes and dreams. Paramount's 1969 screen version used a different story.

THE PRODUCERS

MUSIC AND LYRICS: Mel Brooks
BOOK: Mel Brooks and Thomas Meehan
DIRECTOR/CHOREOGRAPHER: Susan Stroman
OPENED: 4/19/01, New York; still running as of December 2005

Mel Brooks swept critics and audiences off their feet in New York with this show, adapted from his 1968 movie *The Producers*. A couple of songs from the movie were incorporated into the otherwise new stage score. The story concerns washed-up Broadway producer Max Bialystock and his nerdy accountant Leo Bloom, who has dreams of being a producer himself. During an audit of Max's books, Leo offhandedly remarks that one could make more money producing a flop than a hit. That flop is "Springtime for Hitler," penned by nutcase Nazi-sympathizer Franz Liebkind. Max and Leo visit him to get the rights, while Franz sings of the beauty "In Old Bavaria" on the roof, accompanied by his pigeons. The two eventually produce the show, financed by Max's wooing of countless rich old ladies ("Along Came Bialy"). Once the show is a go, the producers look for the worst cast ever, and in a surprisingly "good" performance, Liebkind wins the role of Adolph Hitler through his audition song "Haben Sie Gehört Das Deutsche Band?" The show is a surprise hit and Bialystock and Bloom are in trouble. All ends well, after a brief prison detour. The original cast included Broadway stars Nathan Lane (Max) and Matthew Broderick (Leo). The director and most of the lead actors from Broadway were in the 2005 movie musical.

RAGTIME

MUSIC: Stephen Flaherty
LYRICS: Lynn Ahrens
BOOK: Terrence McNally, from the novel by E.L. Doctorow
DIRECTOR: Frank Galati
CHOREOGRAPHER: Graciela Daniele
OPENED: 1/18/98, New York, a run of 834 performances

Ahrens and Flaherty's *Ragtime* takes its book from the popular novel by E.L. Doctorow about the immigrant experience. A stellar cast, including Audra MacDonald and Brian Stokes Mitchell, helped propel the Broadway run. Set at the turn of the 20th century, this musical has a large cast with many interwoven storylines as the characters move from the time of horse-drawn carriages into the modern age of the automobile. This dense plot pits poor immigrants side by side with Henry Ford, Booker T. Washington, Admiral Perry and J.P. Morgan. Ragtime pianist Coalhouse Walker Jr. eventually tries to start a revolution to win equal rights for African-Americans. His attempt for justice leaves him and his men surrounded by the police in the Morgan Library, which he plans to blow up if his demands are not met. He dies in a firefight, but not before he rallies his men to action with the anthem "Make Them Hear You."

THE RINK

MUSIC: John Kander
LYRICS: Fred Ebb
BOOK: Terrence McNally
DIRECTOR: A.J. Antoon
CHOREOGRAPHER: Graciela Daniele
OPENED: 2/9/84, New York; a run of 204 performances

A rundown roller rink is the site of this Kander & Ebb musical. A dreamy show, past and present flow together as a mother and daughter relive their lives as they deal with the pending demolition of their rink. The action takes place from about 1950 to 1970, but the show does not try to be a realistic portrayal of these times. It is, rather, a symbolic celebration of life and renewal. Liza Minelli starred as the daughter, Angel, with Chita Rivera as her mother, Anna. The two reminisce about the mother's longtime suitor Lenny (Jason Alexander), who always wore his heart on his sleeve, proposing to Anna in "Marry Me."

THE ROAR OF THE GREASEPAINT—THE SMELL OF THE CROWD

MUSIC, LYRICS AND BOOK: Leslie Bricusse and Anthony Newley
DIRECTOR: Anthony Newley
CHOREOGRAPHER: Gillian Lynne
OPENED: 5/16/05, New York; a run of 231 performances

The Roar of the Greasepaint—The Smell of the Crowd was another allegorical musical in the same style as the previous Anthony Newley-Leslie Bricusse *Stop the World—I Want to Get Off*. Here the writers were concerned with the weighty theme of playing the Game, which covers such universal topics as religion (the supplicating ballad, sung by Cocky, "Who Can I Turn To?" is addressed to God), hunger, work, love, success, death, and rebellion. Leading the cast were Cyril Ritchard as Sir, representing ruling class authority, and Anthony Newley as Cocky, representing the masses who submissively play the Game according to the existing rules, no matter how unfair they are. Each day the two come together to play the Game. With the upper hand at the beginning, Sir sings joyfully "On a Wonderful Day Like Today." Sir and Cocky find it in their best interests to mutually help each other in the end. The musical folded in England without a London opening.

1776

MUSIC AND LYRICS: Sherman Edwards
BOOK: Peter Stone
DIRECTOR: Peter Hunt
CHOREOGRAPHER: Onna White
OPENED: 3/16/69, New York; a run of 1,217 performances

Sherman Edwards' background as a high school history teacher made him a perfect choice to bring the American Revolution to the Broadway stage. Edwards' characters of our heritage leap off the page and their real personalities shine through—the disliked firebrand John Adams, the quiet lover Thomas Jefferson, and the witty Benjamin Franklin, among many others. The cast consists of largely the signers of the Declaration of Independence. We see the fierce debates over states rights, individual autonomy and slavery in the hot Philadelphia days of that defining year. Much of the dialogue is taken verbatim from memoirs and letters of the actual participants. *1776* is not a typical musical with large dance numbers and many songs. It allows ample time for the plot to unfold, and often there are very long breaks with no music as the delegates debate in Congress. Jefferson and congressmen of the North want an anti-slavery clause put in the new constitution, but Edward Rutledge of North Carolina vehemently opposes this. He points out that the practice of slavery positively affects the economy of the entire country, from "Molasses to Rum" to slaves. The 1972 movie, directed by Hunt, kept many of the original Broadway actors including William Daniels (Adams), Ken Howard (Jefferson) and Howard Da Silva (Franklin). A Broadway revival was staged in 1997.

THE SOUND OF MUSIC

MUSIC: Richard Rodgers
LYRICS: Oscar Hammerstein II
BOOK: Howard Lindsay and Russel Crouse
DIRECTOR: Vincent J. Donehue
CHOREOGRAPHER: Joe Layton
OPENED: 11/16/59, New York; a run of 1,443 performances

For many youngsters growing up in the 1960s, *The Sound of Music* was the first musical they ever saw, either via the long-running 1959 Broadway version (the third-longest run for Rodgers and Hammerstein) with Mary Martin, or primarily via the Oscar-winning 1965 film version with Julie Andrews. The latter became the top grossing film of its time. *The Sound of Music* was adapted from Maria Von Trapp's autobiographical *The Trapp Family Singers* and a German film version of the story, which Mary Martin was convinced would provide her with an ideal stage vehicle. Her husband, Richard Halliday, and producer Leland Hayward secured the rights and, initially, they planned to use only the music associated with the famed singing family plus one additional song by Rodgers and Hammerstein. Eventually, the songwriters were asked to contribute the entire score, and they joined Halliday and Hayward as producers. This was the only Rodgers & Hammerstein musical with a book not written by Hammerstein. The play is set in Austria in 1938. Maria Rainier (Martin), a free-spirited postulant at Nonnburg Abbey, takes a position as governess to the seven children of the widowed and autocratic Captain Georg Von Trapp. She loosens things up around the house, which has been run like a battleship since the death of the children's mother. Maria teaches the children to sing and play, and the sound of music melts the Captain's heart. After Maria and the Captain fall in love and marry, their happiness is quickly shattered by the Nazi invasion, which forces the family to flee over the Alps to Switzerland. Often mistaken for a real Austrian folksong, Richard Rodgers' "Edelweiss" is sung memorably, and patriotically, by the Captain, accompanied on guitar.

WICKED

MUSIC AND LYRICS: Stephen Schwartz
BOOK: Winnie Holzman, based on the novel *Wicked: The Life and Times of the Wicked Witch of the West*
    by Gregory Maguire
DIRECTOR: Joe Mantello
CHOREOGRAPHER: Wayne Cilento
OPENED: 10/30/03, New York; still running as of December 2005

Stephen Schwartz's return to Broadway came with *Wicked*, a hit from 2003. Based on Gregory Maguire's 1995 book, the show chronicles the backstory of the Wicked Witch of the West, Elphaba, and Good Witch of the North, Glinda (Galinda), before their story threads are picked up in L. Frank Baum's *The Wonderful Wizard of Oz*. At times a dark show, the original production was characterized by lavish sets and had a stellar cast, including Kristin Chenoweth, Idina Menzel, Norbert Leo Butz, and Broadway immortal Joel Grey. Elphaba, as the Witch of the West, has taken up social justice as her cause, and is wreaking havoc upon the land of Oz. The Wizard tries to dissuade her from her efforts, instead relying on her new found celebrity, as he has. It's really "Wonderful."

THE WILD PARTY

MUSIC, LYRICS AND BOOK: Andrew Lippa
DIRECTOR: Gabriel Barre
CHOREOGRAPHER: Mark Dendry
OPENED: 2/24/00, New York; a run of 54 performances

Two productions of *The Wild Party* hit New York in 2000, the unsuccessful Broadway show by Michael John LaChiusa, and the Off-Broadway, and now more popular Andrew Lippa musical. Both were based on the scandalous 1928 poem by *The New Yorker* editor Joseph Moncure March. This jazz age drama, depicting a night of decadence and debauchery at a party thrown by lusty showgirl Queenie and her abusive lover, vaudeville clown Burrs, was inspiration for Lippa's accomplished score. Kate, a semi-reformed hooker, arrives with her squeeze, Mr. Black. Queenie and Black have an attraction for each other, and Black lets her know of his intentions in "I'll Be Here."

WISH YOU WERE HERE

MUSIC AND LYRICS: Harold Rome
BOOK: Arthur Kober and Joshua Logan
DIRECTOR AND CHOREOGRAPHER: Joshua Logan
OPENED: 6/25/52, New York; a run of 598 performances

It was known as the musical with the swimming pool, but *Wish You Were Here* had other things going for it, including a cast full of ingratiating performers, a warm and witty score by Harold Rome, and a director who wouldn't stop making improvements even after the Broadway opening (among them were new dances choreographed by Jerome Robbins). The musical was adapted by Arthur Kober and Joshua Logan from Kober's own play, *Having a Wonderful Time*, and was concerned with a group of middle-class New Yorkers trying to make the most of a two-week vacation at an adult summer camp in the mountains (of upstate New York or New England). Determined to woo a nervous Teddy, Pinky slowly and insidiously puts his moves on in "Relax."

WOMAN OF THE YEAR

MUSIC: John Kander
LYRICS: Fred Ebb
BOOK: Peter Stone
DIRECTOR: Robert Moore
CHOREOGRAPHER: Tony Charmoli
OPENED: 3/29/81, New York; a run of 770 performances

Based on the 1942 Hepburn/Tracy MGM movie, *Woman of the Year* chronicles the lives of Tess Harding, a nationally recognized TV news reporter, and Sam Craig, a comic strip cartoonist. They fall in love and marry. Tess is about to win the "Woman of the Year" award, but her overbearing nature drives Sam away. They eventually reconcile, and Sam tells her that "Sometimes a Day Goes By" when he doesn't think of her, but those days are few and far between when they are apart. On Broadway the show starred a couple of baritones, Harry Guardino and Lauren Bacall.

WONDERFUL TOWN

MUSIC: Leonard Bernstein
LYRICS: Adolph Green and Betty Comden
BOOK: Joseph A. Fields and Jerome Chodorov
DIRECTOR: George Abbott
CHOREOGRAPHER: Donald Saddler
OPENED: 2/25/53, New York; a run of 559 performances

Wonderful Town reunited the creative team that made 1944's *On the Town* so successful: Bernstein, Comden and Green, and director George Abbott. Set in New York, this show is not a sequel; rather it is based on the hit Broadway play *My Sister Eileen*, which itself was based on Ruth McKinney's semi-autobiographical *New Yorker* short stories. The show was conceived as a showcase for Rosiland Russell as Ruth. Ruth and Eileen are two sisters making their way in Greenwich Village, originally from a small town in Ohio. Ruth is a writer, and Eileen is…well, pretty. As Ruth chases the story, Eileen is chased by suitor after suitor. Ruth's editor, Bob Baker, comes over to apologize for being curt with Ruth, and Eileen immediately falls "a little bit in love" with him. Baker doesn't need a lot of drama, though. He thinks he's looking for "A Quiet Girl." After a raucous night with seven amorous, Conga-dancing Brazillian naval cadets that lands Eileen in jail, all is well in the end. Eileen finds a singing career, after realizing that Ruth and Bob love one another. Bob knows "It's Love" as well, even though Ruth is hardly a quiet girl. A revival came to Broadway in 2002, with Donna Murphy as Ruth.

YOU'RE A GOOD MAN, CHARLIE BROWN

MUSIC, LYRICS AND BOOK: Charles Gesner; Andrew Lippa added songs for the Broadway revival
DIRECTOR: Joseph Hardy
CHOREOGRAPHER: Patricia Birch
OPENED: 3/7/67, New York; a run of 1,597 performances

With Charles Schultz's appealing comic strip "Peanuts" as a general inspiration, Clark Gesner created a musical out of events in "a day made up of little moments picked from all the days of Charlie Brown, from Valentine's Day to the baseball season, from wild optimism to utter despair, all mixed with the lives of his friends (both human and non-human) and strung together on the string of a single day, from bright uncertain morning to hopeful starlit evening." A familiar sight to readers of the comic, Charlie Brown's attempts at getting his kite to fly act as a metaphor for success in life in "The Kite." The show was an Off-Broadway hit. It moved to Broadway for a brief run in 1971. For the 1997 Broadway revival, Andrew Lippa wrote two new numbers.

A FELLOW NEEDS A GIRL
from *Allegro*

Lyrics by OSCAR HAMMERSTEIN II
Music by RICHARD RODGERS

Copyright © 1947 by Richard Rodgers and Oscar Hammerstein II
Copyright Renewed
WILLIAMSON MUSIC owner of publication and allied rights throughout the world
International Copyright Secured   All Rights Reserved

I'M A BAD, BAD MAN
from *Annie Get Your Gun*

Words and Music by
IRVING BERLIN

© Copyright 1946 by Irving Berlin
Copyright Renewed
International Copyright Secured   All Rights Reserved

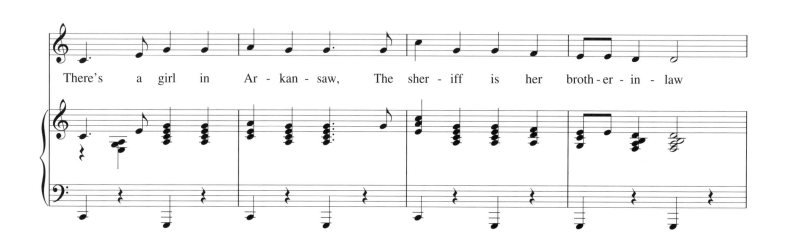

OTHER PLEASURES
from *Aspects of Love*

Music by ANDREW LLOYD WEBBER
Lyrics by DON BLACK and CHARLES HART

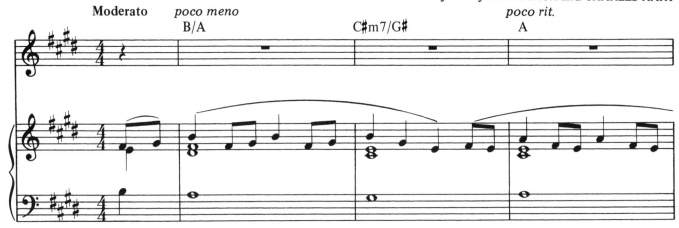

Other pleasures, and I've known many... After-

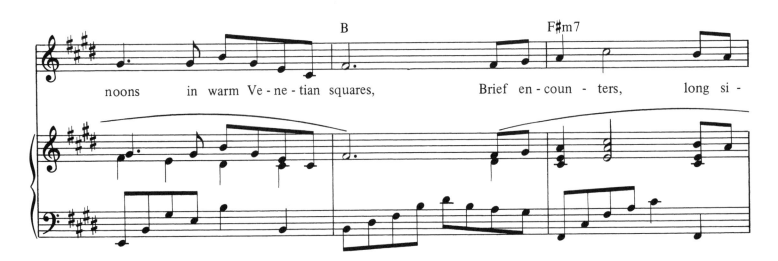

noons in warm Venetian squares, Brief encounters, long si-

© Copyright 1989 Andrew Lloyd Webber assigned to The Really Useful Group Ltd.
International Copyright Secured   All Rights Reserved

I'M NOT WEARING UNDERWEAR TODAY
from the Broadway Musical *Avenue Q*

Music and Lyrics by ROBERT LOPEZ
and JEFF MARX

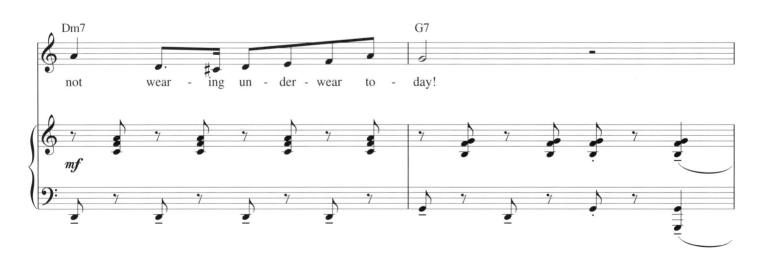

Copyright © 2003 Only For Now, Inc. and Fantasies Come True, Inc. (administered by R&H Music)
International Copyright Secured   All Rights Reserved
For more info about Avenue Q, visit www.AvenueQ.com

FANTASIES COME TRUE
from the Broadway Musical *Avenue Q*

Music and Lyrics by ROBERT LOPEZ and JEFF MARX

This ensemble has been adapted as a solo for this edition.

Copyright © 2003 Only For Now, Inc. and Fantasies Come True, Inc. (administered by R&H Music)
International Copyright Secured   All Rights Reserved
For more info about Avenue Q, visit www.AvenueQ.com

*Truncated in this solo edition. See vocal selections for the complete section.

WHAT DO YOU DO WITH A B.A. IN ENGLISH

from the Broadway Musical *Avenue Q*

Music and Lyrics by ROBERT LOPEZ
and JEFF MARX

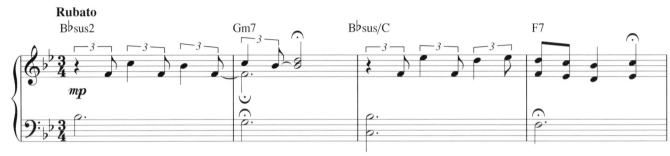

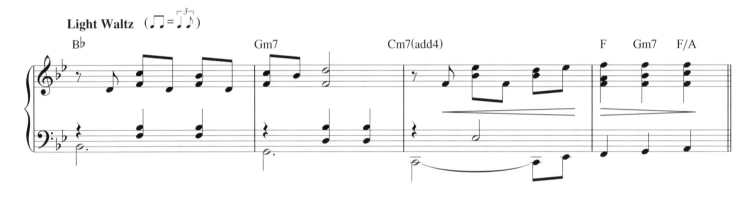

PRINCETON:
What do you do___ with a B. A. in Eng - lish?

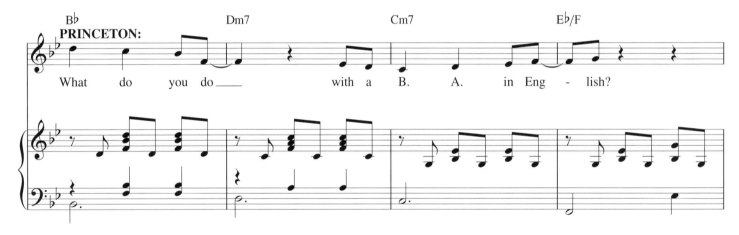

What is my life___ going to be?

Copyright © 2003 Only For Now, Inc. and Fantasies Come True, Inc. (administered by R&H Music)
International Copyright Secured   All Rights Reserved
For more info about Avenue Q, visit www.AvenueQ.com

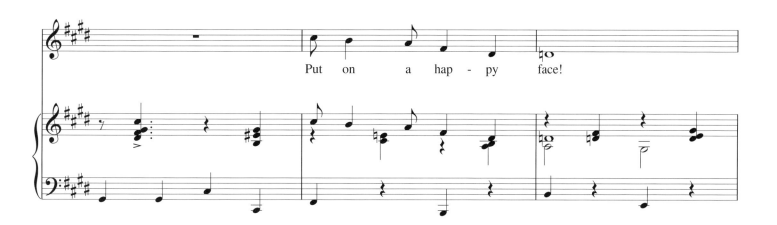

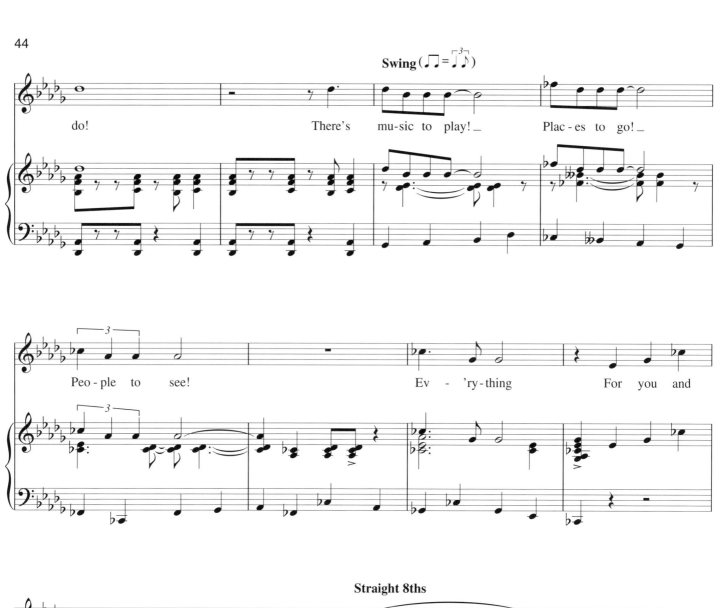

WAITIN' FOR THE LIGHT TO SHINE
from *Big River*

Words and Music by
ROGER MILLER

Copyright © 1985 Sony/ATV Songs LLC and Roger Miller Music
All Rights Administered by Sony/ATV Music Publishing, 8 Music Square West, Nashville, TN 37203
International Copyright Secured   All Rights Reserved

MASCULINITY
from *La Cage aux Folles*

Music and Lyric by
JERRY HERMAN

© 1983 JERRY HERMAN
All Rights Controlled by JERRYCO MUSIC CO.
Exclusive Agent: EDWIN H. MORRIS & COMPANY, A Division of MPL Music Publishing, Inc.
All Rights Reserved

I WONDER WHAT THE KING IS DOING TONIGHT

from *Camelot*

Words by ALAN JAY LERNER
Music by FREDERICK LOEWE

BRING ME MY BRIDE
from *A Funny Thing Happened on the Way to the Forum*

Words and Music by
STEPHEN SONDHEIM

Copyright © 1962 by Stephen Sondheim
Copyright Renewed
Burthen Music Company, Inc., owner of publication and allied rights throughout the world
Chappell & Co., Sole Selling Agent
International Copyright Secured   All Rights Reserved

Ensemble lyrics have been slightly adapted for this solo edition.

* optional cut to **

THE RIGHT GIRL
from Follies

Music and Lyrics by
STEPHEN SONDHEIM

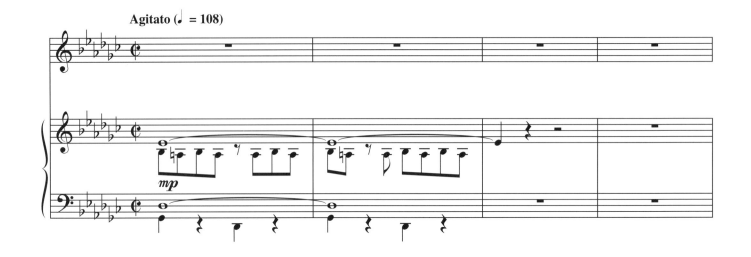

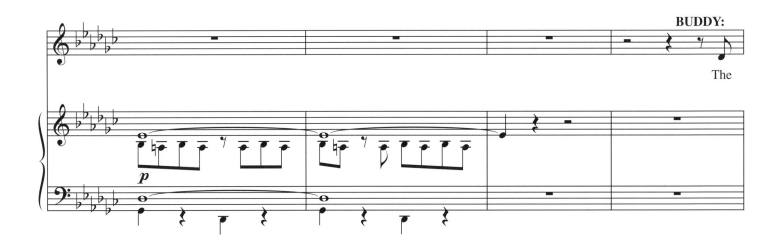

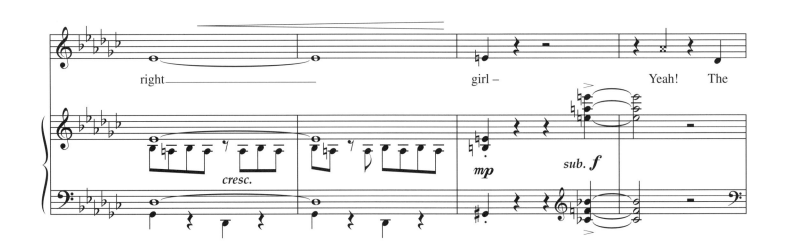

Copyright © 1971 by Range Road Music Inc., Jerry Leiber Music, Mike Stoller Music, Rilting Music, Inc. and Burthen Music Co., Inc.
Copyright Renewed
All Rights Administered by Herald Square Music, Inc.
International Copyright Secured   All Rights Reserved

80

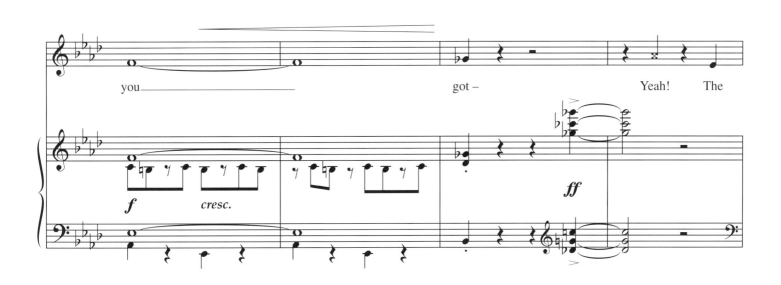

82

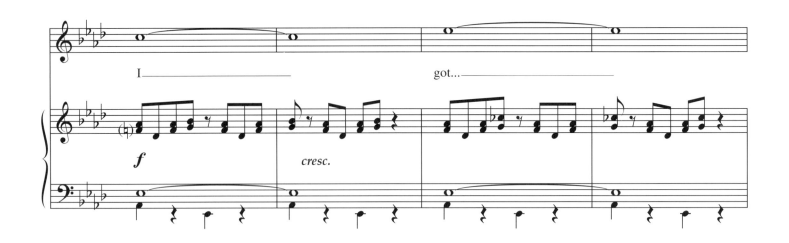

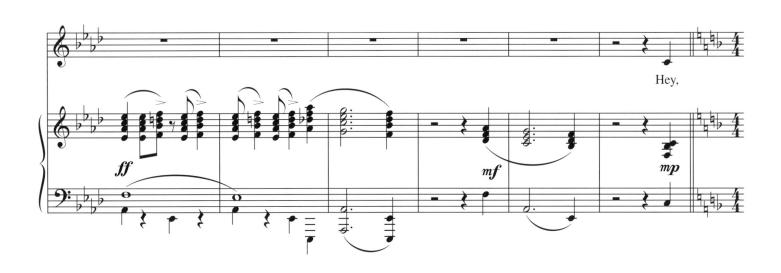

GREASED LIGHTNIN'
from *Grease*

Lyric and Music by WARREN CASEY
and JIM JACOBS

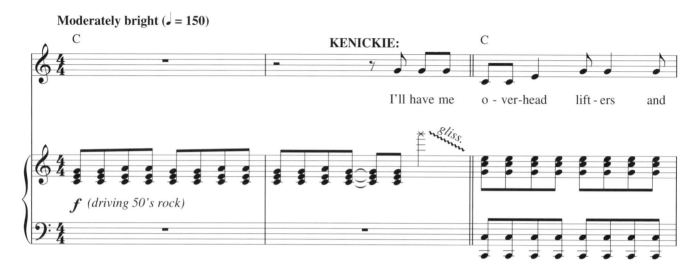

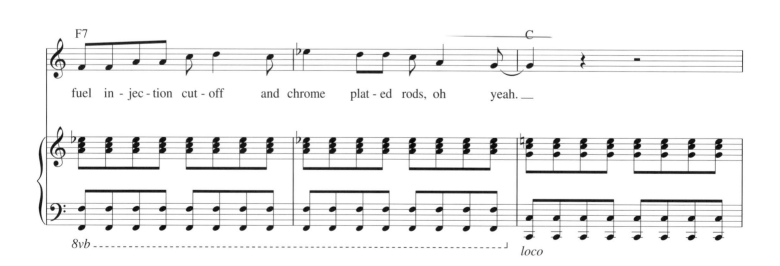

© 1971, 1972 WARREN CASEY and JIM JACOBS
© Renewed 1999, 2000 JIM JACOBS and THE ESTATE OF WARREN CASEY
All Rights Administered by EDWIN H. MORRIS & COMPANY, A Division of MPL Music Publishing, Inc.
All Rights Reserved

THOSE CANAAN DAYS
from *Joseph and the Amazing Technicolor® Dreamcoat*

Music by ANDREW LLOYD WEBBER
Lyrics by TIM RICE

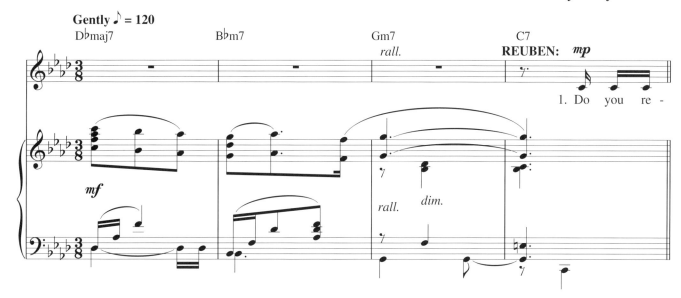

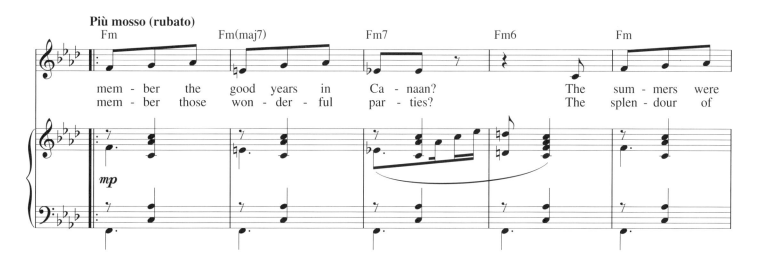

© Copyright 1975 Andrew Lloyd Webber assigned to The Really Useful Group Ltd.
Copyright Renewed
International Copyright Secured   All Rights Reserved

SHOULDN'T I BE LESS IN LOVE WITH YOU?
from *I Love You, You're Perfect, Now Change*

Lyrics by JOE DiPIETRO
Music by JIMMY ROBERTS

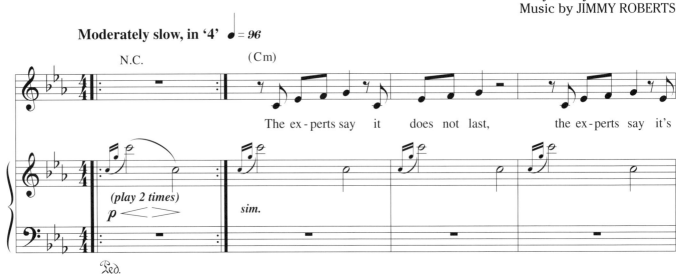

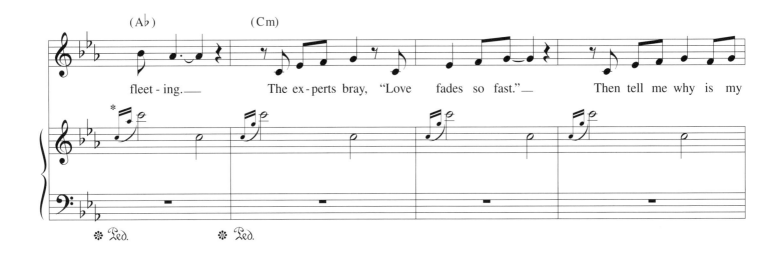

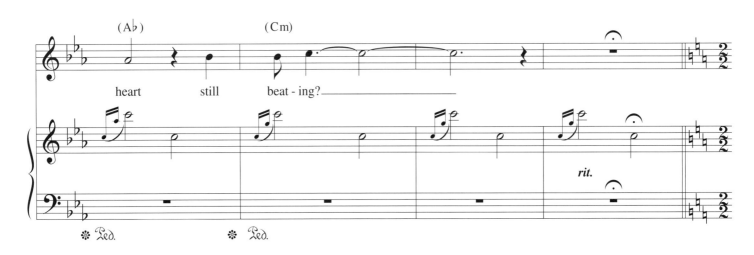

*(Grace notes in measures 5 and 9 differ from previous grace notes)

Copyright © 1996 by WILLIAMSON MUSIC
International Copyright Secured   All Rights Reserved

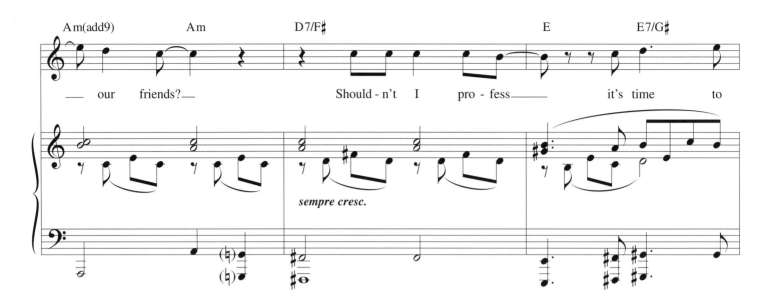
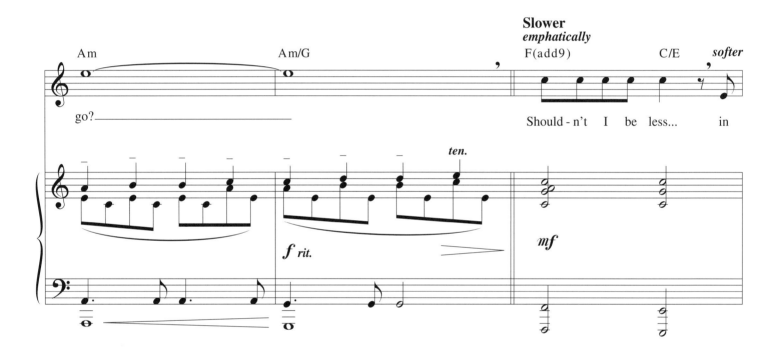
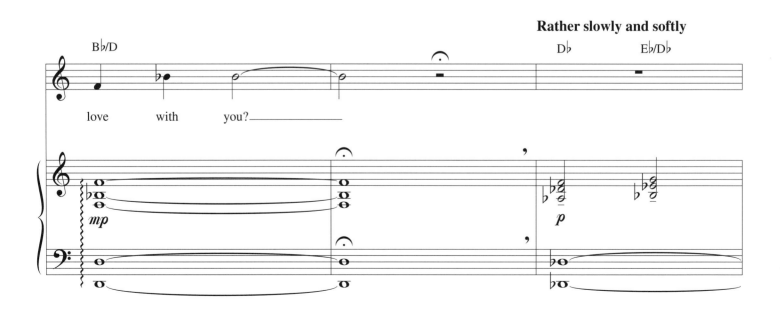

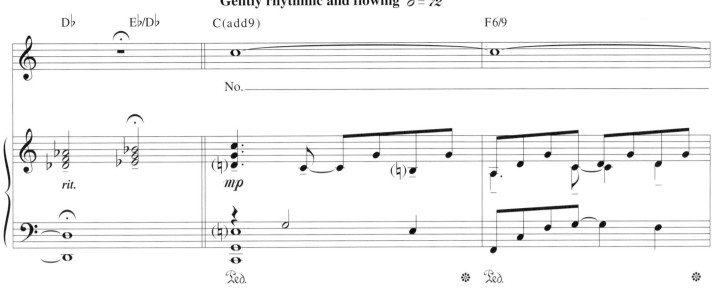
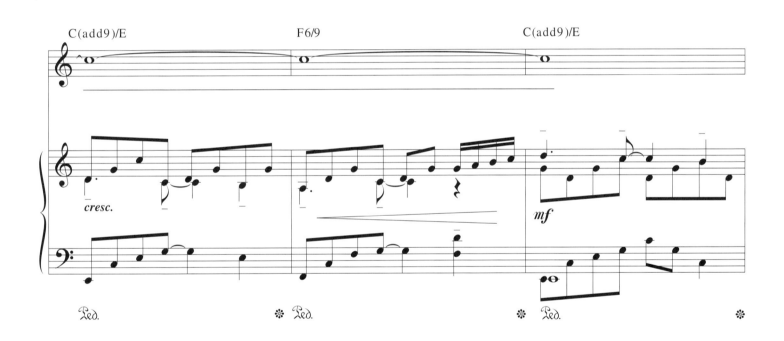
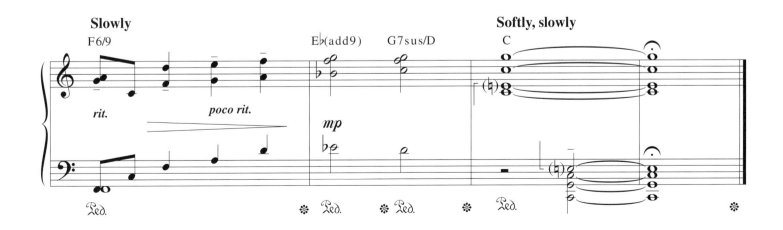

WHAT CHANCE HAVE I WITH LOVE?

from the Musical Production *Louisiana Purchase*

Words and Music by
IRVING BERLIN

© Copyright 1940 by Irving Berlin
Copyright Renewed
International Copyright Secured   All Rights Reserved

THERE'S NO REASON IN THE WORLD
from *Milk and Honey*

Music and Lyric by
JERRY HERMAN

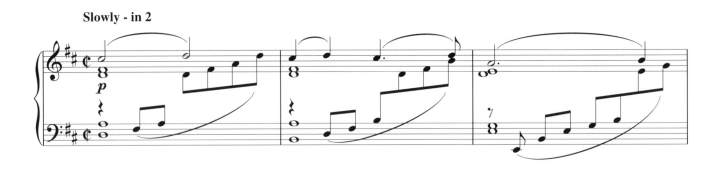

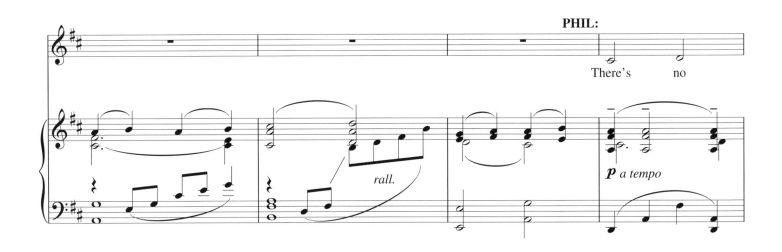

© 1961 (Renewed) JERRY HERMAN
All Rights Controlled by JERRYCO MUSIC CO.
Exclusive Agent: EDWIN H. MORRIS & COMPANY, A Division of MPL Music Publishing, Inc.
All Rights Reserved

YA GOT TROUBLE
from Meredith Willson's *The Music Man*

By MEREDITH WILLSON

HAROLD HILL *(spoken introduction)*: Either you're closing your eyes to a situation you don't wish to acknowledge or you are not aware of the calibre of disaster indicated by the presence of a pool table in your community.

This song has been adapted as a solo for this edition.

© 1957, 1958, 1966 (Renewed) FRANK MUSIC CORP. and MEREDITH WILLSON MUSIC
All Rights Reserved

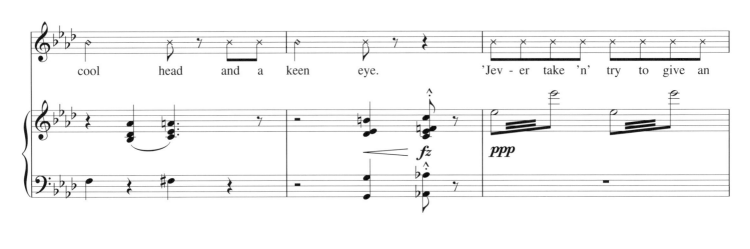
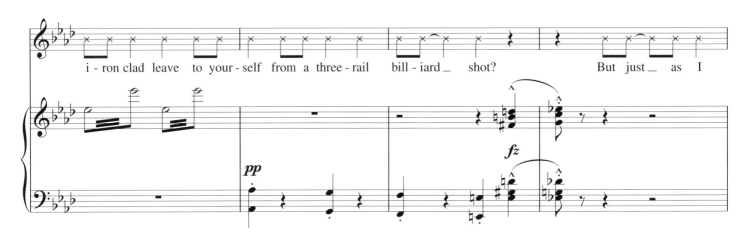
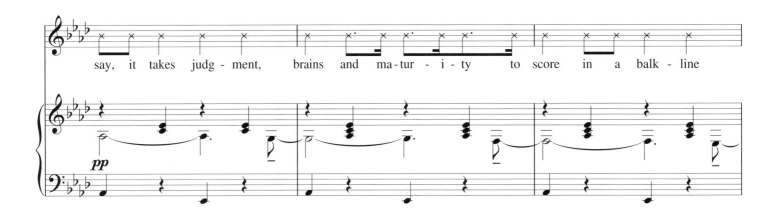
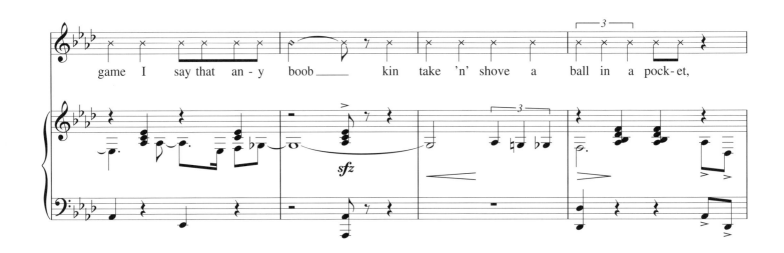

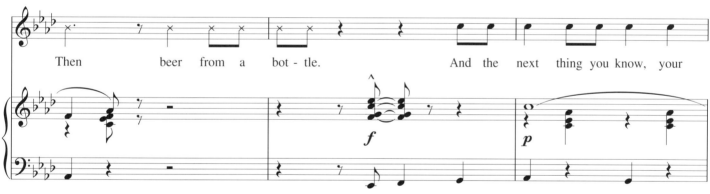

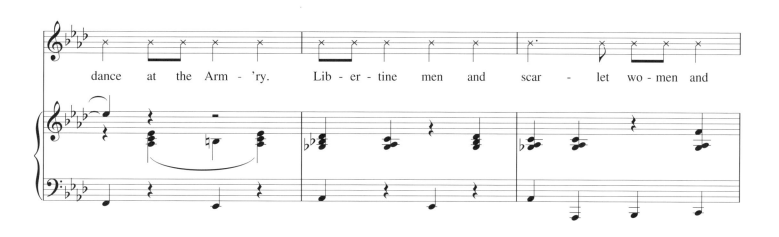
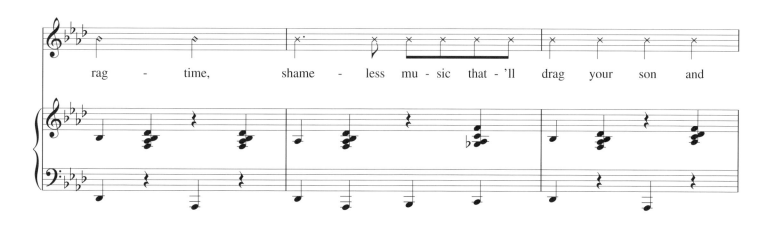
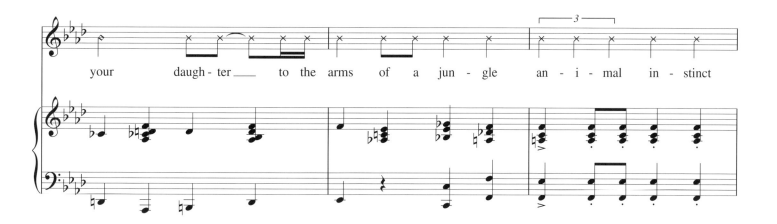

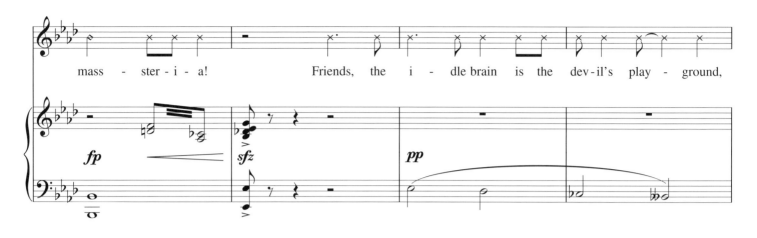
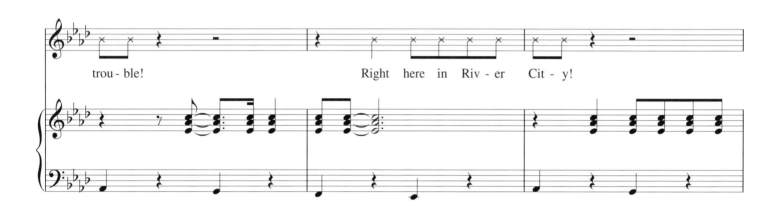
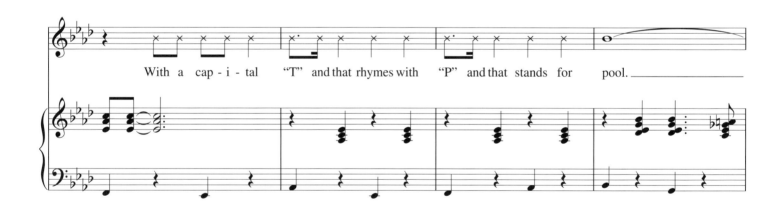
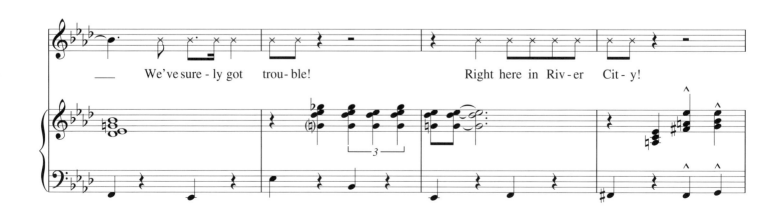

This song is an ensemble number in the show, adapted as a solo for this edition.

© 1979 KAY-GEE-BEE MUSIC LTD. and EMI VIRGIN MUSIC LTD.
All Rights for the United States and Canada Controlled and Administered by EMI VIRGIN MUSIC, INC.
All Rights for the World excluding the United States and Canada Controlled and Administered by EMI VIRGIN MUSIC LTD.
All Rights Reserved   International Copyright Secured   Used by Permission

*Second time, for audition purposes, cut to **

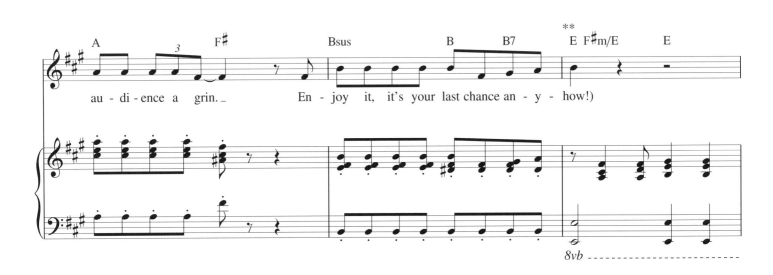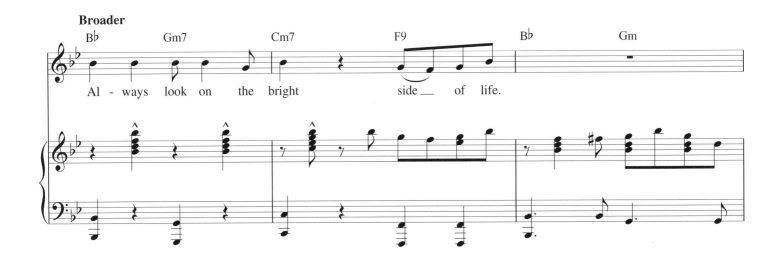

GET ME TO THE CHURCH ON TIME
from *My Fair Lady*

Words by ALAN JAY LERNER
Music by FREDERICK LOEWE

DOOLITTLE: *There are drinks and girls all over London, and I have to track 'em down in just a few more hours.*

I'm get-tin' mar-ried in the morn-in'!

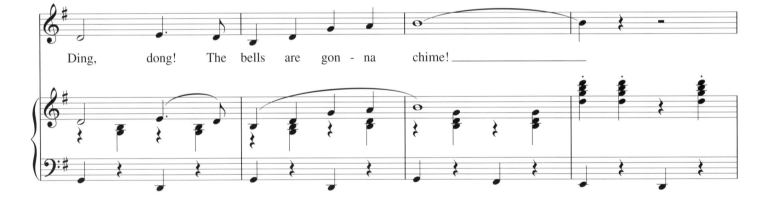
Ding, dong! The bells are gon-na chime!

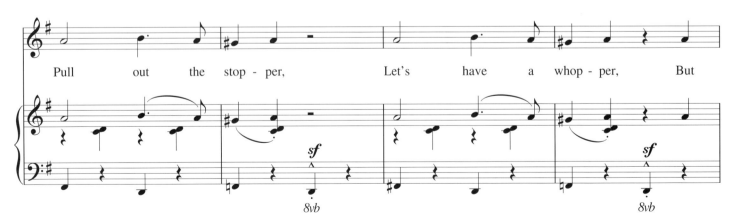
Pull out the stop-per, Let's have a whop-per, But

Copyright © 1956 by Alan Jay Lerner and Frederick Loewe
Copyright Renewed
Chappell & Co. owner of publication and allied rights throughout the world
International Copyright Secured   All Rights Reserved

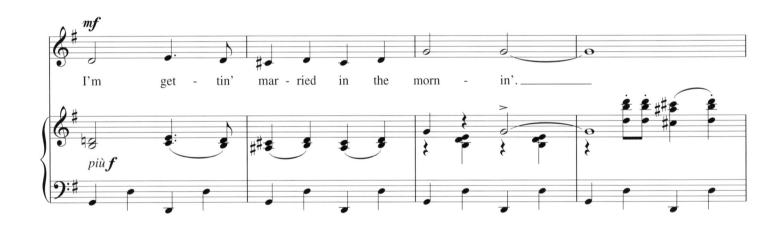
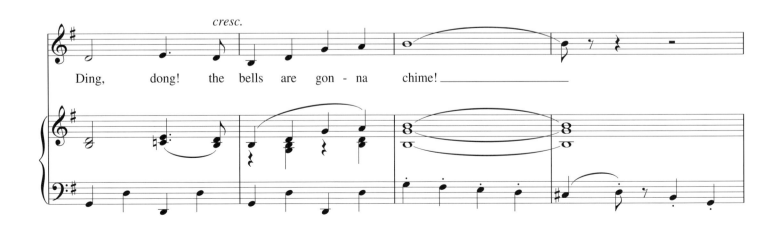

WITH A LITTLE BIT OF LUCK
from *My Fair Lady*

Words by ALAN JAY LERNER
Music by FREDERICK LOEWE

Copyright © 1956 by Alan Jay Lerner and Frederick Loewe
Copyright Renewed
Chappell & Co. owner of publication and allied rights throughout the world
International Copyright Secured   All Rights Reserved

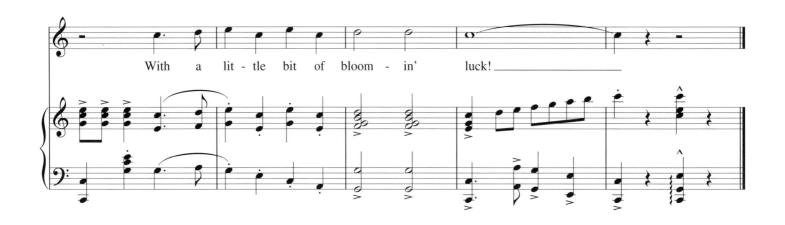

ALONG CAME BIALY
from *The Producers*

Music and Lyrics by
MEL BROOKS

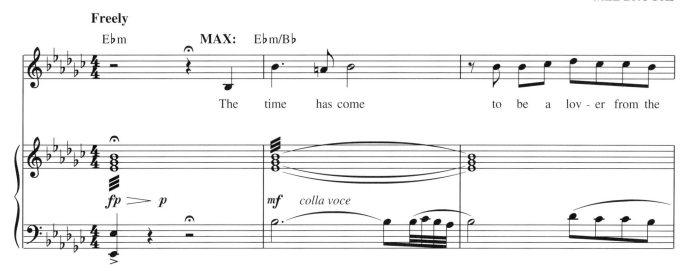

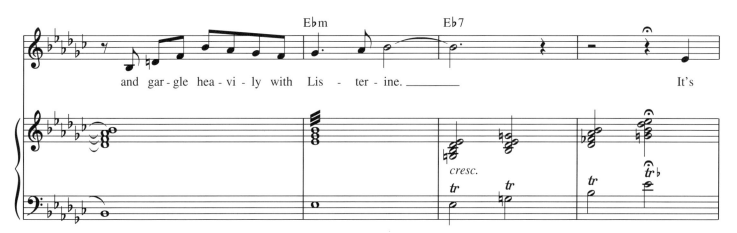

This ensemble has been adapted as a solo for this edition.

Copyright © 2000 Mel Brooks Music (BMI)
All Rights Reserved   Used by Permission

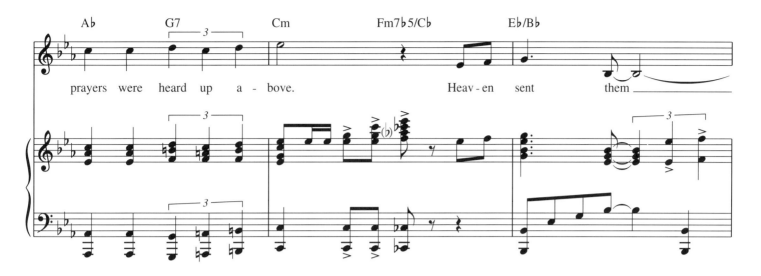

IN OLD BAVARIA
from *The Producers*

Music and Lyrics by
MEL BROOKS

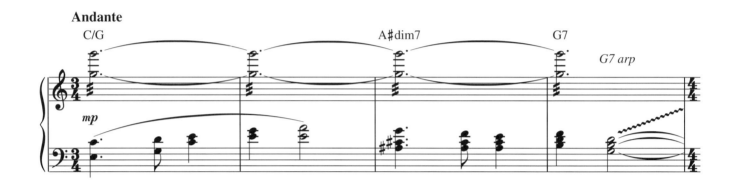

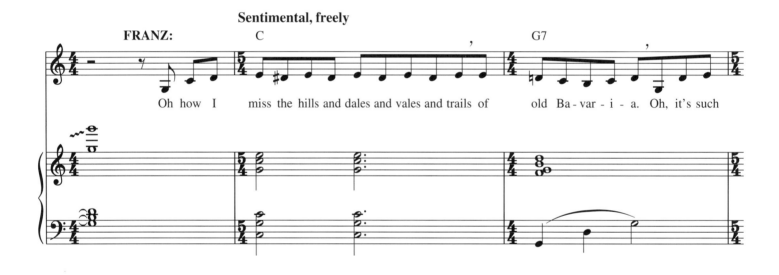

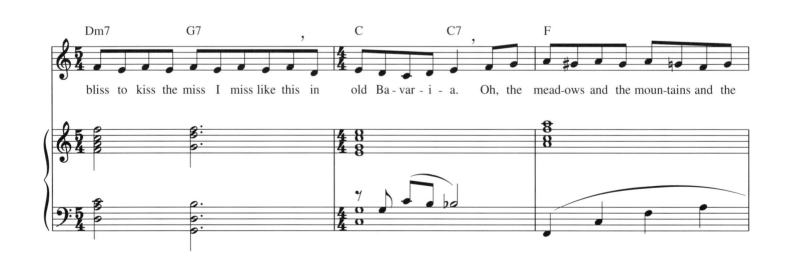

Copyright © 2000 Mel Brooks Music (BMI)
All Rights Reserved   Used by Permission

HABEN SIE GEHÖRT DAS DEUTSCHE BAND?
(Have You Ever Heard the German Band?)
from *The Producers*

Music and Lyrics by
MEL BROOKS

WAND'RIN' STAR
from *Paint Your Wagon*

Words by ALAN JAY LERNER
Music by FREDERICK LOEWE

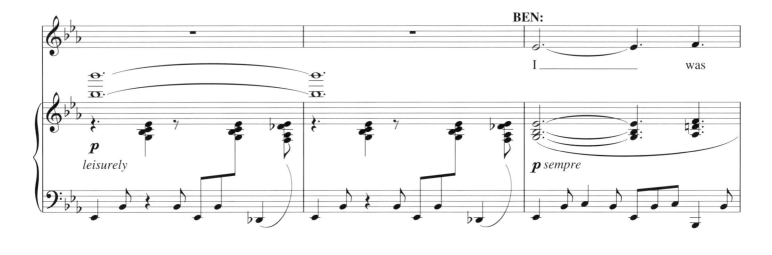

The song was originally notated in triplets in 4/4, changed to 12/8 throughout for clarity.

Copyright © 1951 by Alan Jay Lerner and Frederick Loewe
Copyright Renewed
Chappell & Co. owner of publication and allied rights throughout the world
International Copyright Secured   All Rights Reserved

MAKE THEM HEAR YOU
from *Ragtime*

Words and Music by STEPHEN FLAHERTY
and LYNN AHRENS

© 1996 WB MUSIC CORP., PEN AND PERSEVERANCE and HILLSDALE MUSIC, INC.
All Rights Administered by WB MUSIC CORP.
All Rights Reserved   Used by Permission

MARRY ME
from the Musical *The Rink*

Words by FRED EBB
Music by JOHN KANDER

Copyright © 1983, 1985 by Kander & Ebb, Inc.
All Rights Controlled and Administered by Bro 'N Sis Music Inc.
International Copyright Secured   All Rights Reserved
Used by Permission

A WONDERFUL DAY LIKE TODAY
from *The Roar of the Greasepaint–The Smell of the Crowd*

Words and Music by LESLIE BRICUSSE
and ANTHONY NEWLEY

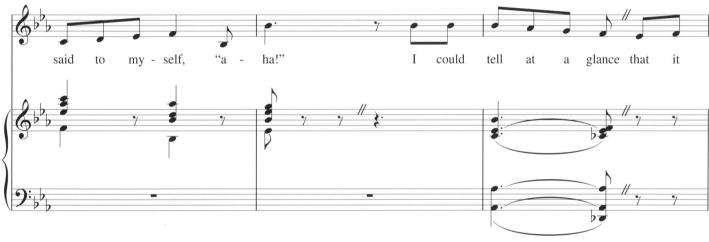

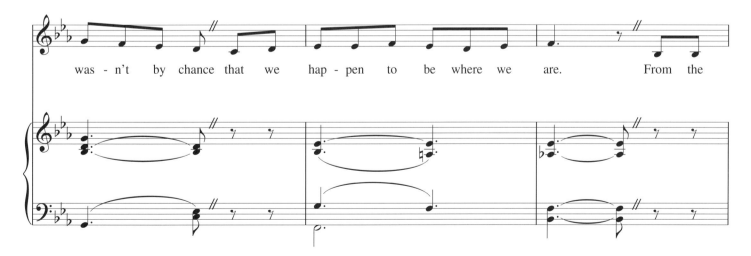

© Copyright 1964 (Renewed) Concord Music Ltd., London, England
TRO - Musical Comedy Productions, Inc., New York, NY controls all publication rights for the U.S.A. and Canada
International Copyright Secured
All Rights Reserved Including Public Performance For Profit
Used by Permission

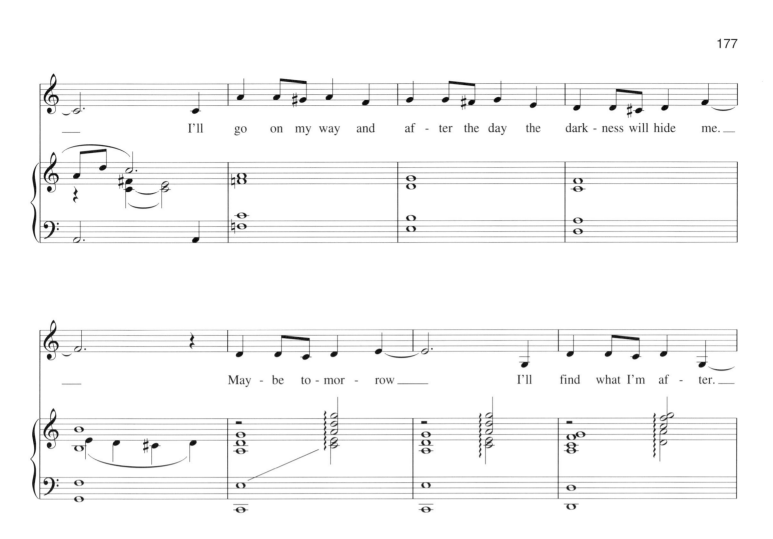

180

MOLASSES TO RUM
from *1776*

Words and Music by
SHERMAN EDWARDS

Copyright © 1964 (Renewed), 1968, 1969 by Sherman Edwards
All Rights Administered by 1776 Music, Inc.
All Rights Reserved   Used by Permission

EDELWEISS
from *The Sound of Music*

Lyrics by OSCAR HAMMERSTEIN II
Music by RICHARD RODGERS

Copyright © 1959 by Richard Rodgers and Oscar Hammerstein II
Copyright Renewed
WILLIAMSON MUSIC owner of publication and allied rights throughout the world
International Copyright Secured   All Rights Reserved

WONDERFUL
from *Wicked*

Music and Lyrics by
STEPHEN SCHWARTZ

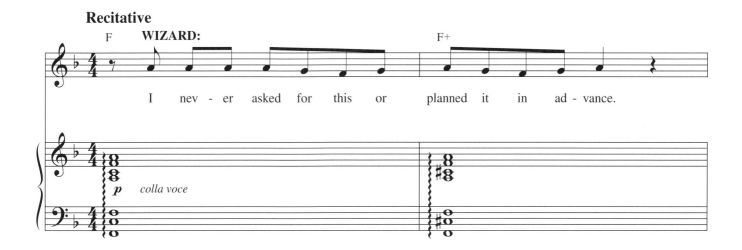

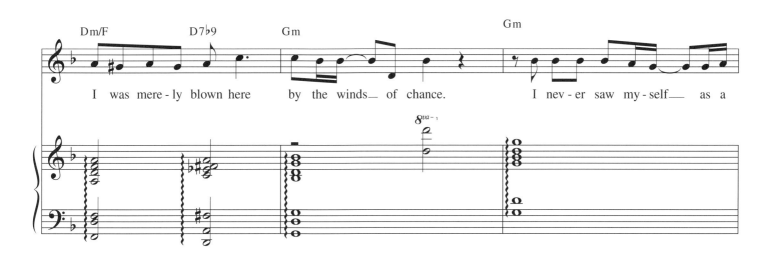

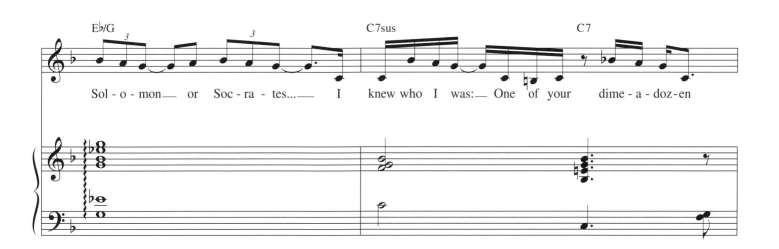

Copyright © 2003 Greydog Music
All Rights Reserved Used by Permission

I'LL BE HERE
from *The Wild Party*

Words and Music by
ANDREW LIPPA

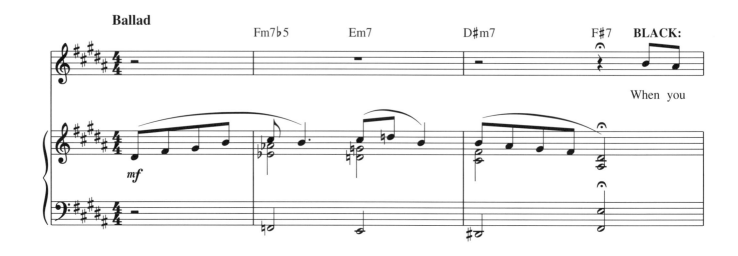

© 1999 Andrew Lippa
All Rights Reserved

RELAX
from *Wish You Were Here*

Words and Music by
HAROLD ROME

The song is really a duet of sorts, with spoken lines of the female character Teddy interjected. Though it can be sung effectively as a solo, Teddy's lines are are retained in this edition for comprehension.

Copyright © 1952 by Chappell & Co.
Copyright Renewed
International Copyright Secured   All Rights Reserved

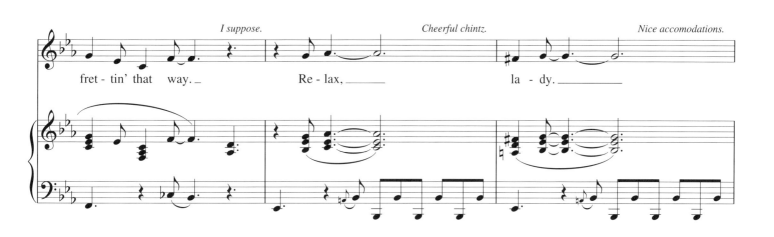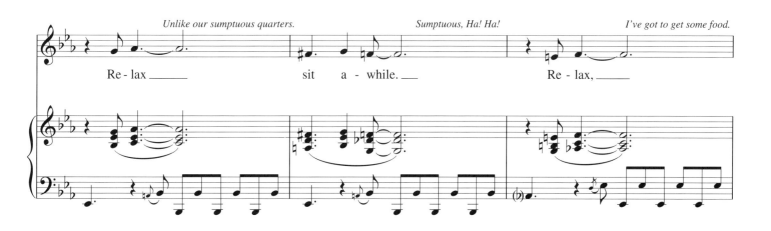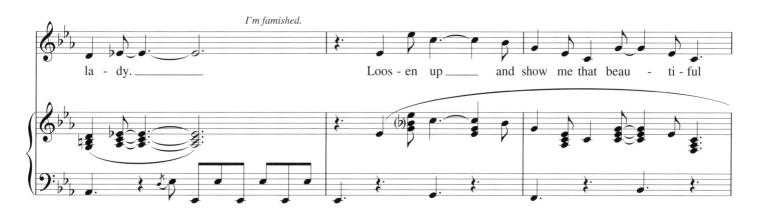

IT'S LOVE
from Wonderful Town

Lyrics by BETTY COMPEN
and ADOLPH GREEN
Music by LEONARD BERNSTEIN

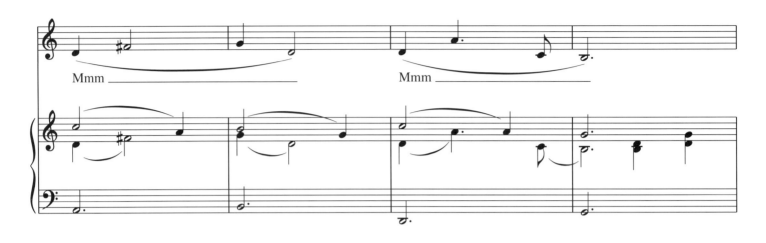

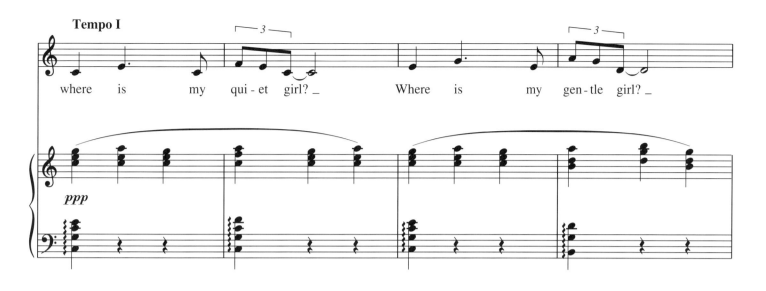

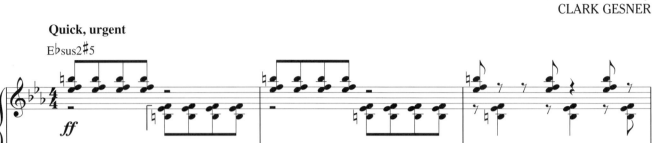

THE KITE
(Charlie Brown's Kite)
from *You're a Good Man, Charlie Brown*

Words and Music by
CLARK GESNER

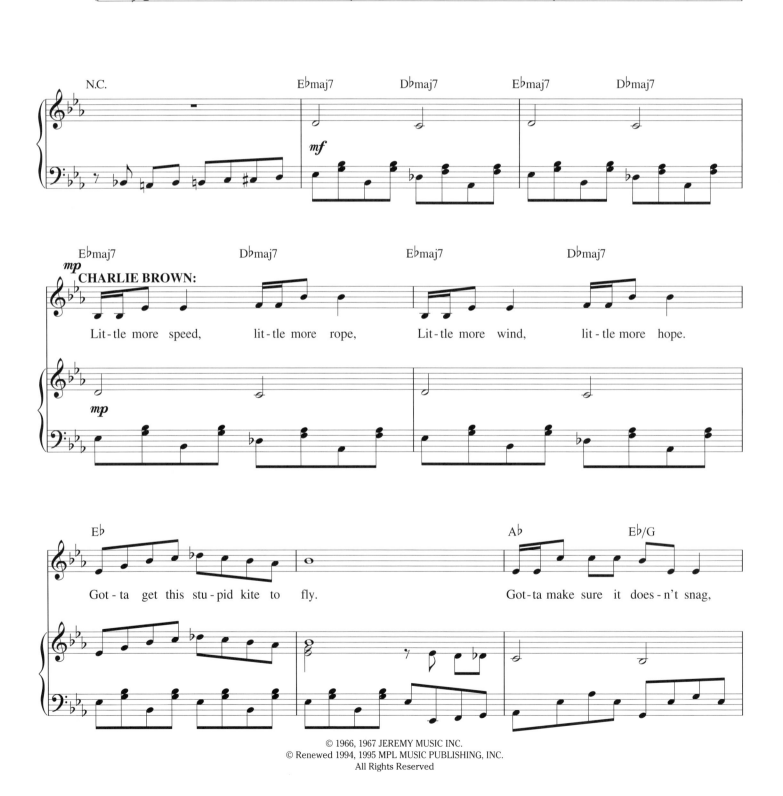

© 1966, 1967 JEREMY MUSIC INC.
© Renewed 1994, 1995 MPL MUSIC PUBLISHING, INC.
All Rights Reserved

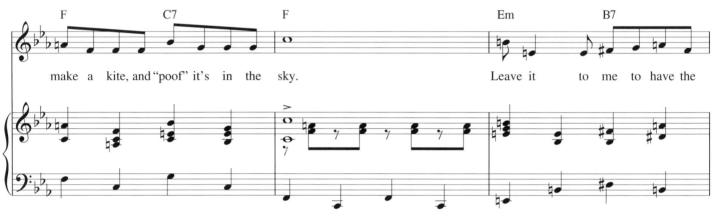
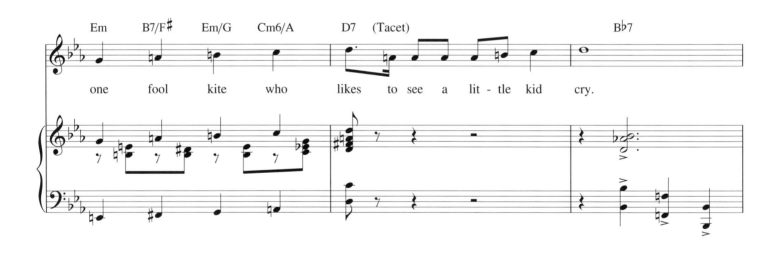
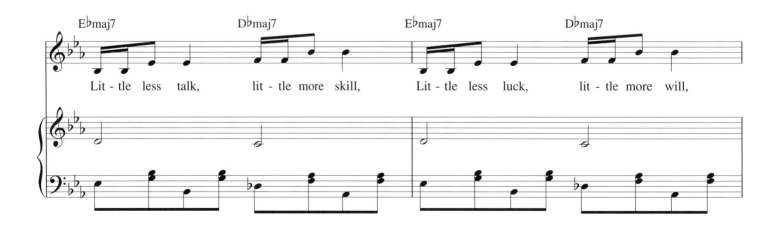

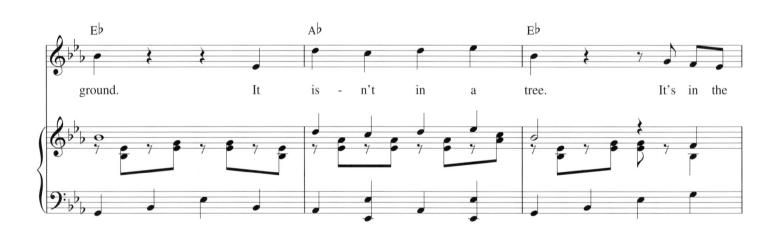